Garage Elegies

Also by Stephen Kessler

POETRY

TRANSLATION

Changing Centuries (poems by Fernando Alegría) 1985
Widows (novel by Ariel Dorfman) 1983
Homage to Neruda (poems by eight Chilean poets) 1978
Destruction or Love (poems by Vicente Aleixandre) 1976

FICTION

The Mental Traveler (novel) 2009

NONFICTION

Need I Say More?: Portraits, Confessions, Reflections (essays) 2015
The Tolstoy of the Zulus: On Culture, Arts & Letters (essays) 2011
Moving Targets: On Poets, Poetry & Translation (essays) 2008

EDITOR

The Sonnets by Jorge Luis Borges 2010

Garage Elegies

STEPHEN KESSLER

BLACK
WIDOW
PRESS

BOSTON

Black Widow Press is an imprint of Commonwealth Books, Inc., Boston, MA. Distributed to the trade by NBN (National Book Network) throughout North America, Canada, and the U.K. All Black Widow Press books are printed on acid-free paper, and glued into bindings. Black Widow Press and its logo are registered trademarks of Commonwealth Books, Inc.

Joseph S. Phillips and Susan J. Wood, Ph.D., Publishers
www.blackwidowpress.com

Author photo: Christina Waters
Cover art: Kay Bradner
Cover design and book production: Kerrie L. Kemperman

ISBN-13: 978-0-9995803-2-5

Printed in the United States
10 9 8 7 6 5 4 3 2 1

The author wishes to thank the editors of the following periodicals, where some of these poems first appeared: *The Arkansas International, Catamaran, Chicago Quarterly Review, Gargoyle, Mission at Tenth, Mission Village Voice, Osiris, Statgelichter* (Germany), and *St. Petersburg Review.*

Special thanks to Walter Martin, Rebecca Taksel, Marc Hofstadter, Carolyn Tipton, Barry Fruchter, Kate Todd, Kay Bradner, and Gary Young for their attentive reading of some of these poems, and for their friendship and encouragement.

IN MEMORIAM

Richard O. Moore   Wanda Coleman   Eduardo Smissen

Contents

Garage Elegies

You old man, it get worse.
YAT KI LAI

Optimism is the death of literature.
ALTA IFLAND

CASSANDRA

With your swampy voice, your electric hair,
rhythm of reeds tideswayed in the rivershallows,
sinuous strings, sidemen on the bank keeping the beat,
you sing bad news with a sound of sweet illusions, of doom
that is not a disaster but merely inevitable, what anyone would
    expect
if they took a deep look at the evidence everywhere, beauty and
    truth
entwined with death, cruelty on the loose, tenderness barely
    enduring
under the lash of chaos muted by coercion—those rules
even the stupid can understand—and out of such murky depths
some lovely myth may rise in song to beggar disbelief.
Those who hear you are bound by a weird spell, swept down-
    stream
from the blue music of their misery through currents of
    unexpected
syncopation, which twist perception, wring the grief-soaked soul
into streams of grateful relief, torrents of pleasure
that move at crosspurposes against the grave eddies of fate.
What are you trying to prove, that what we believe
to be given is bound to flee, that from devastation flows
creation unfettered by mere facts, that emanations of
    incomparable sound
transcend defeat, floating into a zone where even tragedy is
    redeemed?
Your prophecy is not lost on me, Cassandra,
your phrasing is too persuasive, your timing
too bittersweet to dispute. I believe you, babe,
whatever the gods, so self-absorbed
as to ignore our sufferings,
have up their sleeves.

WE ARE NOT MANY

We are not many. In fact we are hardly any.
I see in the surrounding swirl of crowds
scarcely a trace of the same species—

these people, familiar as they appear,
are more than strange, they seem somehow alien
life forms come to remind me it is I who am odd man out

of these games on screens, these movies in the other rooms,
this lounge full of people playing with their phones,
this need to be unceasingly entertained.

Just give me a ten-ton SUV and a TV wide as a whole wall
and a girl with breasts and a job and a house and a portable
machine to think my thoughts and remember what I forgot—

these things will permit me to exist as long as I have
this code imprinted in my forehead, this chip
on my increasingly sloped shoulder.

SHRINE

The house is becoming a shrine to my dead friends.
Wanda haunts the walls with memorabilia, immortalia,
Austin's collages, posthumous poster, a low-budget broadside.
Bill Elmore's *Sardines and Limes* has gained in grave beauty
since he died in a fire in his trailer a few months ago.
And now Eduardo, his two masterpieces here more gorgeous
and mysterious by the day now in the few days
after his death. *The Spanish Chair* sprouts the trees of its legs
upside down into the south of France, a map of that coast
background above bold blue, black, and gold-leaf bands;
Diversion's greenish horizontal waves more turbulent,
its lone bird perched on the back of the same chair right side up
but adrift on an ominous ocean, grim sky edged in gold—
these images are physical facts
whose artifice lifts them into an afterlife
more alive now than their makers—
paradox of the artifact.
Bill was an excellent painter but a diffident man,
looking over his shoulder at Rembrandt
and finding his own work wanting.
Wanda the poet aggressively asserting her greatness
against the wealth of obstacles stacked in her path.
Eduardo the lighthearted rascal willing to scavenge and steal
whatever in order to advance his mischief.
All oddly come and gone, all at the after party with Greg and
    Fred,
Alastair and Phil, Denise and Fernando and Dick Brickner.
The list grows longer and longer, the trail of tears muddier
and cloudier, the dust more dense
with what little is left of them. And we're next,
that's what's so weird, being an absence
whose only evidence is its leftovers. These words

one day as even now may give me something
lacking in "real life," achingly erotic
and offering some relief or release of feelings
one is embarrassed to confess unless ironically
in meta-postmodernist menopause where the avant-garde
surrenders in despair. Why not admit you have nothing to say
and say it anyway and let the tears fall where they may
in mourning for the suddenly missing,
who seem to demand more than they did before.

GARAGE ELEGIES 1

The garage elegies are composed without elegance
in runny ink resembling motor oil,
black as if in mourning for losses of the increasing years
when friends and loves keep disappearing, so we must grieve
and keen, imagining there's something we can do,
and this is what we're doing.
My confidence in what endures endures, and yet
my disbelief is unsuspended, abandoned in pursuit
of more demonic muses who lash me onward with their whiplike
    locks
and rough caresses, teasing the last juice out of me whispering
Give it to me baby, and how can I refuse.
Here I am watched by Lincoln and Lin Yutang,
Milosz and Bukowski leaning against the cardboard boxes
loaded with evidence of my transgressions
shelved in plywood compartments above the maple tables
built for my office in the Floating World.
The rug is thin and faded but it covers the concrete floor,
this rocker salvaged from the shop of an antique dealer
decades ago, its worn arms oiled with my hands' long touch
as I sat learning to do nothing and listen.
And this is what we're reduced to
once everything has been said,
the last house sold, the endless refrains redundant,
the motorcycles roaring up the coast long gone
and the sirens behind them quiet,
on the quietest Sunday of the year
when the nation worships at the Church of Football
and only the anomalous are not mesmerized by their televisions.
I will claim these cobwebs
and my wife's bras drying atop the washing machine
and the bicycle whose tires are a little low

and the garden tools hanging in the corner
and the collage-in-progress on the side door
and the office supplies tucked into big shelves
over any religious ritual and its corporate sponsors.
Your brand here, my agent would advise,
but I have no agent and nothing to sell,
and instead of entering the din with my absence of amplification
I spend my spare time typing, on antique typewriters,
epic letters to the select or writing by hand,
on pages unlikely to be seen by anyone,
notes of no known use.

GREEK PHILOSOPHERS

The punched-out busts of Greek philosophers
marble noses knocked off by barbarians
or maybe their own empire on its way down
look me in the eye from a book cover
as if to say *You too will end up*
like us only less so.

DEEP IN THE HEART OF TOPANGA CANYON

for Mike and Sarah

Before dinner is served and the dancing begins,
before the vows are pronounced and the families merged
and the friends descend with their blessings,
the ghosts of gamblers and gangsters, escorts,
hippie dropouts, boy scouts and Hollywood homos,
including some of our close relations,
will hover lovingly over the landscape
making the case for marriage,
butterflies fluttering in the sagebrush,
and the October sky itself will speak
of heatwaves and floods and temblors and wildfires
held at a safe distance for the duration
so the guests can groove under the imported palms
and the planted succulents can absorb the warmth
of so many lovers come to witness the ritual,
surrounding chaparral dangerously dry,
oaks and eucalypts down the canyons raising their arms and
    alarms
in praise of sun and rain, the hills themselves rumbling
with seismic excitement at what is about to happen:
a man and a woman made one with words,
a smashed glass to scatter any bad news
though chance and luck will turn every way
as they do for everyone as time unwinds,
but legally linked and bound in spirit,
teamed up as souls entangled in the same long game,
lifting their histories to a new plane,
flying right out of their former lives
into an arc whose shape they'll create as they soar

and swoop and bank and glide and loop
the eternal loops of wedded bliss and distress,
these pilots of their own flight
will find what they make of themselves
for better and worse, with toughness and care
and whatever it takes to make for tender landings,
because everyone knows we know so little
we must make it up as we go along, like artists,
and a kiss is such an excellent place to start,
such a sweet way to declare solidarity,
to enter the stream of oneness,
the whitewater of a lifetime,
a lifelong tale of everyday adventure
in a tongue they share and each one composes uniquely,
just as this incantation invokes a mixture of emotions
fit for the occasion, the protagonists' folks
saying so long and welcome home at the same time,
the bride and groom riding waves of arrival
as they say goodbye to whatever was
and embark on a journey wild and strange
whose twists and turns will rhyme with the roads
we drove to be here to toast the newly joined,
to feast our eyes on the faces, the flowers,
the ironwork and tiles so cool with their Spanish accents,
and to smell the mountain air and sip the sparkling wine
and savor the food and feel the force of song.

FROM THE MINIBAR

for A.

The frosty blond glaze on my fumé blanc
is nothing next to your noir Bourbon
but echoes of grains and grapes are rustling
everywhere we listen
and with each sip we taste
what terroir we share,
traces of urbane sidewalks
with hints of the coughs of tubercular
nightingales and gurgling of Roman fountains,
detectives' fedoras' felt
stained by their newspaper-page-turned
fingertips, and of course the lipstick
of all those lovely dames
without mercy or the decency
to leave us be. We are bemused
by their mixed signals, and so we try
to warble in their honor yet they refuse
to be seduced no matter how insanely
seductive our sweet & sour nothings
and nothingnesses muttered luckily
in their delicious and oh so sensitive ears.
So here we are, bereft,
bearing our gifted burdens
across every street where the pedestrians
look the other way.

HANGING IN SAN JOSÉ

In the parking lot
Outside the Sharks' rink I wait
For my baby with her skates.

Middle of a drought—
Sprinkling the cement plant's crushed rock
To keep down the dust.

Hundreds of Hondas in the lot
Across the street behind the chain link—
Acres of desolation.

Below Mount Umunhum,
California Roofing Co.
Passed by traffic on Tenth Street.

A taco truck rolls up Tenth Street;
The groundskeeper raises a dust storm
With his leafblower.

SURELY OBLIVION HAS MUCH IN STORE

Surely oblivion has much in store.
The custom sunglasses deepen the bifocal
darkness ahead as we drive headlong
into a setting sun. Up close the words
seem to mean more, while the farther removed
the less weight they carry even as they float
lightly in the afterlife, which is nothing
but a trace of what we were.

THE MUSES ARE BITCHES AND THE LINE
BREAKS ARE GIVING YOU A HARD TIME

The muses are bitches and the line breaks are giving you a hard
    time.
Those lovely gals batting their long lashes and lashing you with
    their leathery tresses
open long closed wounds whose old gashes reveal traces
of forgotten arguments with estranged others now lost in their
    own translated embraces.
They trade in multiple tongues like promiscuous interpreters
    who can speak
only as spoken through, like you, transmuted past your own
    silence into speech
or kisses you almost wish you understood.
Are movies more cruel, the stars too large, too unreachable to
    believe,
or are the babes in your balcony meaner still in their ceaseless
hauntings and unexplained consolations that never quite find
    their angle of repose.
You are reduced to recording their calls and transcribing what
    you can decipher
of their elusive swerves, ruinous and renewing, everpresent and
    ephemeral
as any one of several remembered faces, ones who reappear
unpredictably in public yet hardly unexpected because there are
    so few.
The same ones play all the roles, rotating
in an endless round of performances, yours.

WHICH OLD POET DO YOU WISH TO BE

Which old poet do you wish to be:
the one who can't quit even though
he has run out of what to say,

the one who keeps on discovering
what is unsayable and tries to say it,

or the one who knows enough
to keep it to himself because
nobody cares anyway.

The neighborhood is teeming
with all three, each kind
remembering what got away,

smells of cafés, produce markets
spilling their mangoes onto the sidewalk,
Italian kitchens just heating up
for the evening rush.

It is Friday, early summer,
and the streets are simmering
with anonymity, the city's gift.

NOTHING LEFT TO SAY

There's nothing left to say
and I must say it.
So many other mouths
have uttered such words
and still we speak,
scrape redundant ink
over white sheets in hope
some stain may stay.
It will end soon
and there'll be nothing
left and yet we keep scratching away
at what we can't touch,
or lost back when
and that's that.
It wasn't so bad to suffer so
for that once-in-a-life,
its indelible impressions,
evidence printed in our skin.
Wasn't this always
why we kept on, in hopes
we might whisper the right
nothings into a certain ear
whose taste will come
to know and be known by us
or the other way round,
our long losses all upside
down by now so who knows
which end is up, or why
go on, and yet we do.

ENDINGS

An ending is when
you know it is over
yet you haven't quite looked
for the last time on what
you loved and so you don't
let go or know how to
but know you must,
the beauty of the beloved truth
is tracked with others' touch,
or worn down with your own,
you pressed it too hard
against you and now
the embrace is done
and the truth gone
while always held
in reserve, and so
in these last late hours
all you understood
to be yours no longer is
and you must go on.

FORMAL POETRY

Letter to Walter Martin composed on a full-page ad in
The New York Times

Walter, like you, I am a lover
of formal poetry, each poem
embodies its own unique form,
as does every muse
and sheet of news.
My new formal
formation and fun
form of expression
is, as you know
from postal unfoldings,
the not quite blank
page with a shape
already impressed
upon it,
and my task is to
find or compose
a complementary
shape to embrace
as my words would
a woman
whatever shape
graces the page,
so that you
as exclusive reader
may caress its most
hidden meanings
and discern
through your simple yet profound
act of attention

what it's about, or what it's all
about, or about how long
we can go on
without
what we
have gone
without
for so
long,
I mean
the sweet
touch
of what
we miss
and the
warm
evenings
and nights
and mornings
of soft skin
for which we
are still
in mornings
of long solo
nights
in mourning,
having had our
fun, our turn
at Adam's curse,
and the lost paradise
of tender lust
long afternoons of 75 degrees
when California was long
and yoga limber the better

to bend to the will
of passion and ecstatic gratification
which led to this fixation
and confession, from your rabbi
confessor, of what his spirit
cannot wrap its faith around,
the inexplicable twists of great
good luck and dirty tricks
of fate, of faded flames
and flamed-out fame
and famous dames
with no mercy who done us
wrong, yet in a double
reverse, she is the very one
to whom we owe our song,
and I sometimes wonder
if I could choose
which I would take
of one or the other, the song
without the dame or the other
way round. I've found
in my long road to no place
on which I find myself
like a prawn on a chessboard
or king in a skillet
that we are cooked
and checked no matter what,
the queens of our dreams
and our hives whose drones
we are don't give a damn
for our distress, they are too
busy tormenting and making demands
of others, pleasing them
and teasing out new meanings

for the cryptic invocations
we are
composing
because we
can't help
what we are
since the
moment those
sexy shapes
on the page
got us by the bardic
hairs on our brows
and made us slaves
of their shapely ways
so that ever since
we have tried to trace
that first grasp
of formal grace
in rhymes of all kinds
and trickier rhythms
than the teachers taught
in order to imitate
the staggering syncopations
of our daze, so struck
and stunned by what we see
and remember seeing once
that we can't stop
its tunes from tumbling
in our brains, and our heads
fill up with astounding sounds
that must be set loose
somewhere, so here we are
following orders
of magnitude and gratitude

for even that much of what
we have lost, and stroke instead
such lines with such instruments
as lend themselves to our absurd
pursuits, which sometimes make us jump
for joy between deeper dives
of grief, and who can say
which is the dream and which the real
relief. That's why I praise
form wherever I find it, or in what
shape on what kind of page
where white space
asks to be stained with song
even if the song is wrong
or the letter is off
so we must improvise the words
and the beat, and imagine the backup
singers, you know those girls,
they egged you on from an early age,
sirens & vixens & coquettes & flirts &
will-of-the-wisps whose willowy
sways & curves & amazing moves
surprised you and made you feel
so good you wanted more
all your life long, and you found words
were the only way to hold those forms
& momentous moments always,
fixing them to fit
whatever page made you a rhyming fool,
so you know those gals are as cruel
as they are cool, but oh so fine
where the sun don't shine
and where it do all the more blue
they make you when they go the way

of the moon, a pale reflection
of that golden light
those never understood nights
left behind in your dazzled
and frazzled mind.
These nights, for best or worst,
are all we have, dear Walter,
and what words we can wring
from what forms we form
for whose sake nobody can say
and they don't even know
but we praise them
anyway.

OLD MAN

The old man in his bathrobe
unshaved for several days
picking up the Sunday paper
from his driveway
is me. Now is time's
turn to play tricks,
just as it was back when
you couldn't see
adulthood coming
because today was so long
even next week was
too remote to imagine.
Tonight is no darker than it is
full of silence sliced by tires,
motors, a stray siren, voices
from a party up the hill.
It is Saturday after all
and we are not yet
refugees, nor displaced
by nature; we are at home,
at peace, at least
on these streets,
and grateful for the roof,
water, electric light.
My father, who was
always turning them off
and who read nothing
but newspapers,
died three decades ago
this date, a number
on the calendar
that happens to recur

and remind. When I bend
to pick up the paper
I think of him.

WATCHING THE NATIONAL LEAGUE
PLAYOFFS AT WEST END PUB

The empty stool at the south end of the bar was meant for my
    butt,
and the amber ale on the coaster atop the concrete counter is the
    right brew
among the multitudes of beers and the Sunday noises of sun-
    down,
dinner hour in October, as families chomp their hamburgers
and children yell and the Giants fans applaud, at the end of the
    second inning,
a routine grounder to third. St. Louis is relieved, for these hours,
of its race wars, as radios report Ebola diagnoses in Dallas,
the planet ravaged by epidemic disasters, mostly man made,
from which baseball is a break. Between innings the commercials
are as stupid as usual as far back as memory echoes
with Gillette blades and Chevy trucks and now prescriptions
for erections on demand and the relief of every symptom
brought to you by watching too much television. At empire's end
the pitchers' motions rhyme with the moves of the waitresses
and the overflowing foam from the pints drawn from the taps
and the dirty glasses turned over in the plastic rack to my left
before being sent back to the dishwashers while there is still
    water.
Soon we will be bathing in our own urine, and washing our
    dishes
with spit, and licking the sweat off each other as in the old days
for something to drink. This is where we are for the duration
and there is nothing to be done but savor the Caesar salad
and pray for rain. But not while the Giants are in the running
and the players are as "gods of the antique wars," as Walt would
    call them,

and as long as they keep on winning and we can stare at the big
    screens
in slow-motion replays that seem, for a moment anyway, all but
    eternal.

THE APPLE PAN

A slice of pie
with ice cream
in the Apple Pan—

nothing could taste
more timeless at
11pm in Los Angeles.

SAM KESSLER

The mug shot dates from 1932,
San Quentin Prison, California.
The convict was arrested in LA,
Possession of a still; a Russian Jew,
Age 52, with balding head, brown eyes,
Dark vest, white shirt, wide tie, and at the knot
A number fastened—52428—
Beneath a dignified and steady gaze.
Occupation: musician, it says here;
He had no other criminal history,
An opportunist in this line of work,
Distilling whiskey in that lean, dry year.
At last, a face to fit the mystery—
My father's missing father. Patriarch.

GARAGE ELEGIES 2

This tropical heat, dry and desertified in the dead of winter,
is the first draft of a drought after a few brief downpours,
and the Saturday silence due to everyone's afternoon at the beach
where the cars are parked from here to over the hill.
This is where the gray heads with no brains come in,
their scratching in befuddled puzzlement,
their unkilled curiosity giving way to unintelligible sighs
long as the cries of lost loves coming in their arms,
those days mysteriously remaining even though long gone
with the brief relief they brought.
Sounds like some kind of dove doodling in the distance
and mingling notes with unnamed songbirds above the street,
their sounds no more gratuitous than these,
an aid to their evolution, to their meeting a mate
and reproducing if only to risk being eaten by free-range cats.
Some of them keep you company sometime,
curled on the faux-leather swivel chair
while you type at the vintage Olivetti,
or rolling on their backs in the warm rough drive
asking to be scratched by a sympathetic hand.
If we are to perish of thirst instead of dying smothered in snow-
     banks
unable to drink our way out because it's too cold and nothing
     melts
to drip relief into the frozen mouth, may the dry lips
at least hallucinate their greatest kisses, and the parched tongue
retaste the sweet spit never to be sipped again.
Let the long knives of those lovely claws draw blood
enough to feed some other lover, and its winelike flavor
make her drunk with final delight,
excitement of the satiated heart.

TRANSLATOR IN HIS LABYRINTH

After several days another long day of corrections,
400 pages plus, *en face*, proofing both languages,
trying out final fine-tunings of what is neverending,
dead poet looking over my shoulder hoping I do no harm,
my muses reaching for the moon to pour its cool beauty
into my approximations, impersonations, personal yet impersonal
interpretations. And now it is near midnight and we are sleepless
with the juice of such transfusion, voice of our common demon
dictating that we don't dream lest we miss some pain
of what passes for the actual. Useless transcription
is the sole recourse this far along the road of uncried tears,
gallons, acre feet of water under the bridges
swept under the rug so no one would witness,
and thus we suffer drought, cars go unwashed,
golfcourses unwatered, toilets unflushed, clouds
wrung out to dry, all because an old man couldn't cry.
A few motors can be heard revving on Mission
but no sirens otherwise in the last while, a semi-
silent night yet not quite quiet enough
to shut the floodgates of ungovernable ink,
the blood of elegiac obituaries the boy of letters must pen
for every friend who fell off the map, flew under the radar
into vast absence, which reverberates, resonates with presences
whose visitations are all but visible, mysterious evidence
everywhere, eloquent and bizarre artifacts. This too
is testimony of a death foretold and a life,
what's left of it, while it lasts—
an almost unwitnessable, formally suspect, raving
dithyramb or ode whose object is elusive, shamelessly
subjective, utterly unpresentable in polite company
and not for sale. How many private arias are being performed

this very hour by those perennially out of reach
of the arms in which they once lay in some distant mist,
and so they sing for want of what they've missed,
the wetness of a mouth, the moist vortex into which they were
    swept
forever if only for a sweet few seconds of transcendence,
following which they were lost, as in translation.

LETTER TO RICHARD MOORE

What good does it do to write
to you? You're dead, even more out of sight
than in your blinded nineties, gone into the Big Fog
streaming over the headlands into the Bay, a vague afterlife
where the renaissance you started with your co-conspirators
still hangs, resonates
and resists what's left
of the greater darknesses, which is a lot.
The papers you couldn't read in those last years
were loaded with bad news, but the invisible books
were still good when you could recall them—
and like Borges you could conjure sonnets,
summon them one line, one rhyme at a time
and retain them until someone arrived
to write them down. So you are on the record
if off the charts, under and beyond the radar, radical spirit
rooted in late light. You worked with faithless faith
to leave a trace that made some sense, some sound order
worthy of your lucidity
to the end.

THE LAST SONG

Ever since you were little the last song you heard
on the clock radio before you were out of bed and off to school,
or blasting from the dashboard on Saturday night as you cruised
with your equally befuddled buddies, or streaming more quietly
from the car radio as you park to take a slow walk in the sun
on the way back from the post office—that last song,
whatever it was, keeps ringing in your head,
which is why you must try to make the music good,
in case it's the last thing you hear in these last elegiac days
when everyone and then some seems to be dropping off,
vanishing from the landscape like creatures you expected to last
    forever
that disappeared. You are going the distance, you'd like to think,
but you know how the breeze changes in a blink and you could
    be gone
with one gust or another, your whitecap rolling back into the
    aquamarine
like all those others in the same springtime
when babies keep being born besides.
The homeless vet with his help-wanted sign on the sidewalk,
the cute cashier who cheerfully tells you to "have a good one,"
the bearded bum on the bus-stop bench in front of the
    laundromat,
girls in their summer shorts eyeing their devices, old men
    mesmerized
by waves all hear different refrains, compose unique soundtracks
they scarcely notice but it plays in the background, a theme they
    breathe
with the day's drama and night's darker pleasures and
    conundrums.
Why you were made to record these numbers is nothing personal
and nobody's business but yours.

DICK'S WAKE

The trouble with everything
is that it's true.
            —Richard O. Moore, 1920–2015

After the stories and the sing-alongs,
your last words knocked into shape at the last minute
to say so-long, the hugs and the handshakes,
I go around the corner to The Cantina
and order a margarita to keep me company
until the family arrives at five. The drink is good
and cold, not too sweet, lime rhyming
with your tart wit, your sharp ear
for the false note, right phrase, rhythm of a line,
perception sifted through intense awareness
into songlike thought—no schmaltz, your signature.
I'm getting ahead of myself, but after you, too late
to point out the distraction of the waitress's bare back,
illusory as it is, yet evidence of what's true, a sign of life
despite your disappearance. I feel (two words
you eschewed) I must report to you, old friend
I met in those years of our common losses.
What counted then was that we knew each other
enough to admit what matters, no matter
how little it meant to anyone else. We know,
through all those solo hours, what it means
to have only shreds of speech
to hold what we had,
to catch what lasts.

IN BETWEEN NOTES

for PJ, after Barzakh

Weeks now since our sparkling waters
with rhyming limes in Vesuvio's
your pages engaged me, ennotebooked with your travels,
languages, heteroformalist wordswarms, reverse translations
and translocations, your sortings, recordings, deracinations,
Franco-Arabian *reportage.* I hear you
but do not follow, my stay-at-home househusbandry grounded
earthily in local turf, barely bilingual, what long and distant roads
we have gone down with pens blazing, burning
holes in our sheets like reckless smokers,
subcatastrophic, witnesses from unsafe removes.
Whose muses could have rolled with us that Christmas,
black ice in white landscape landing us miraculous
in a Greyhound not a Porsche bound for Los Angeles?
How routes rewrite their maps is our life story, so separate
and yet somehow the same, poetry the beam of the lighthouse
coming around again, again and again, redundant as all get-out
yet inevitably necessary and essential.
Each time I read a book of yours I spring into song,
how bad is that? All those missed metaphors,
those drinks under the bridge, too late to return
those calls, those sirenic whoops, those wails over the waters,
we are almost as lost as the others
yet we proceed, twin brothers experimenting in distinct identities.
It was coincidence that synchronized our boyish destinies,
route-canaled our bipolar muses (those gals again,
will they never cease to lash us with their tongues?)
into careenings of ecstatic distinction.
We have met, split, tripped, flipped, skipped
more towns than we can recall or return to,

had kids, got old, all but sobered up,
and here we are again all the same.
Will disaster catch us—has it?—
or are we graced?

GARAGE ELEGIES 3

Phil Levine, the tough guy from Detroit, is gone.
His levelheaded down-to-earth crypto-romantic lyric narratives,
musical, intelligible and moving, not intellectual exercises
but necessary elegies and invocations,
are an antidote for so much static in the present atmosphere.
His book he signed to me, *The Bread of Time*,
discarded by the Danbury Public Library,
is by my bed but I am in the garage
with Barak the silky sweet black cat from next door
curled on the chair he has taken for his,
and with other departed friends.
I'm sick of listening to myself,
of spinning the wheel in search of the winning number,
of spinning my wheels in the quicksand of solipsism,
the same inner spiral of contemplation that goes nowhere
while out there the absurd world with its wars
despairs disasters epidemics and redeeming pleasures
wheels and careens spewing its fumes and perfumes.
The little poster with Phil's face printed for his reading on the
    coast
more than a decade ago
peeks out from behind the office supplies,
pulled from the box of pictures that were once
the sprawling collage on the corner walls of my office,
now the playroom of a ten-year-old.
I seem to be still playing as I was then,
only the room has changed, and the baseball cards
exchanged for other artifacts.
And something still compels me to spill
words in search of the spell that will spell relief.

GARAGE ELEGIES 4

How sick of obituaries do you have to be
before you can retire from writing them—
and then, as Amber asked, who will do yours?
Eduardo drops off the map, then Dick Moore,
the intensely alive disappearing one by one,
but death comes in waves, wiping out the riders time and again.
You are a specialist in this, the catching from a discrete distance,
the tracing of resurrection after the fact, Easter and Passover
    aside,
all miracles void, what's real insurmountable and astonishing
    enough.
Whom to channel with so many lost spirits at large?
Every card dealt appears to speak a small fortune.
April Fools? You must be joking. The tricks should be so brief,
one day is insufficient even for a false start.
Richard, is that you? Trying to turn me into a philosopher?
You know I'm barely a lyricist, my lyre in the shop
having its strings changed, you can hear it from here—
no ideas in strings. No theory, no matter
what the physicists say. It's you and me, dude,
what remains of what we had to say over dinner all those times,
over blind sandwiches in the diner around the corner from Death
    Row,
over my kitchen table those wifeless nights,
our gossip about the famously forgotten fading into the fog,
what we've witnessed and shared over red wine
mostly gone except for these shreds.
Abstractions flutter in the atmosphere,
flying toward the islands of lost truth, a world floating far off.
Yet here we are, still yakking like old ladies who know less
than they let on, more than enough to go around,
and then some. Or was it verse we drank, well, sipped

from the same casks, drunk on what we couldn't quite contain.
I wish you could see the whisk broom stuck in the dustpan
   handle
hanging on the wall above the washing machine,
a couple of flies circling between here and there,
the row of rags hung on the rail by the steps to the back door
and the cat door *sans chat.* I wish you could see anything
now that your blindness is extinguished and your story spreads,
sub-Joycean in the dead of day.
The dark will come quick enough,
no need to obscure or obfuscate,
to scapegoat the skateboarders for scraping up the street
or the transients next door for their entrepreneurial ingenuity,
trading in what-all to make ends meet.
We traffic in language, scarcely more or less tangible,
your book timed to coincide with your dying,
good marketing move for somebody ninety-five.
Your bass voice, or was it baritone,
echoes in the afterlife.

LONG FRIENDS

Why do the long friends last best?
Some kid we played ball with early on
returns ages later as an arts administrator,
a nonprofit nature saver, retired high school teacher,
or the student poet grows up to be a poet,
who would've thought? But there it is
and the ties still bind despite the forked paths
that led so far apart. Lost people don't come back.
But then agendas overlap, times oddly coincide,
the stars align and you are reciting ancient lines
at a reunion, or run into each other on some street.
These meetings can't be planned, they happen
because chance demands it, and connections hold.
Time turns us into memory machines
working after hours to recover
whatever touched us once.

HOUSEHOLD WORDS

Looking over the last edge, the world's
desiccated West, toward the encroaching Orient—
entrepreneurial migrants making their way
into the dustbowls of opportunity,
separating salt from the indifferent ocean,
pumping snow from buried cities back East into the suffering
    Sierras,
catching hurricanes in remote-controlled aircraft to dump
bucket by bucket onto the desert, river guides leading walking
    tours
to interview evolving fish finding their land legs—
I hang close to home and make the most of domestication,
my travels recorded notably and held in cartons
on the elegiac shelves of the garage where in lieu of power tools
office supplies fortify my sagging manhood. So it is
in this aged condition that I take the last steps into eternity
on weakening knees, last legs for brisk walks
in a crisp breeze after a day at the desk doing nothing
more useful than communing with an old friend or two
in letters whacked out on a classical yet operational artifact,
a Royal portable, acoustical as the day is long
and life so brief as to vanish with other impossibly gone
beings persuasively present so lately as to linger forever,
household names privately famous to one Lone Ranger
of remembering. The infinite horizon of perpetual disappearance
is Tennysonian only insofar as it recedes indefinitely,
tempting Ulysses to keep going. I will stay here,
post-adventurous, until the last mystery
is wrung from the mundane, last revelation
mined from the nothing-doing.

LATE LUNCH

These graveyards along the coast have great views,
perfect settings for posthumous picnics with the departed,
their tastebuds' sensitivities intensified by the long fasts of the
    afterlife
and absence of visitors before you arrive and spread your late
    lunch
on the slabs with their names and dates.
The strawberries are sweet, like the mouths of the loves
that won't be kissed again unless in some eternally returning
    rerun
of the great romance before the hatred set in,
but it was a gift for a few minutes.
Now under the eucalyptus a calm contentment can be felt
floating up from underground like a balm for the undeceased,
the days all the more delicious like these cheeses softly spread
on this fresh bread still warm from the bakery
under the spring sun arcing gracefully west,
a warm breeze strangely angling in from the ocean
while the red wine with the twist-off top breathes
in the whiskey glasses you've brought.
Sip, then, after you've toasted the ones
so simply sleeping here after all the exhausting days;
they're grateful for your being alive and present
to remind them what it was like.

GARAGE ELEGIES 5

What gall, what bile in the guts of the bride, so beautiful other-
      wise,
gives her a stomachache that won't stop, like chronic grief
for the ongoing—a human condition beyond relief.
A pedicure may take the mind off pain,
foot bathed and massaged by sensitive hands
which paint the nails whatever shade you please.
The ache is thus eased, for the time being,
and for the nothing that follows.
We trade in what we can, in whatever's left
after the tax collector takes his cut,
and the accountant, the broker, the doctor
whose specialty is the most expensive machinery,
the insurance company and the bounty hunter.
Once everyone's paid off, the stripped patient peels off
the paper gown and slips back into her wedding dress
for a night on the town.
Who thinks about this? Who muses the afternoon away
as the world burns and the bums stand with their sad signs on
      the sidewalks,
and cops stake out the pharmacy parking lots watching for
      shoplifters?
When the prescriptions expire, the lethal injections objected to
by the providers, the last words said, last meals cleared from the
      cells,
the man in the black hood goes home to play with his kids.
The newlyweds raise hell in the honeymoon suite.
The kids on the playground are protected from harm
by electric collars around the offenders' necks—
come too close to the chainlink and be shocked.
But in the timeless nightclub anything goes,
all's fair, especially the faces of the babes

and the dark smiles of the Don Juans
and the angelic shoulders of the cigarette girls
who exist now only in myth, or in old movies.
The bride is distracted from her complaint
by images streaming all night into her suite.

GARAGE ELEGIES 6

Remember the summer night you parked Sinatra's car?
It was uniquely orange, Italian,
he had to import his mechanic to maintain such an elite
    machine.
Mia, his mate at the moment, climbed gracefully out of the
    bucket seat
as you opened the passenger door of the sleek coupe.
You were nothing but a teenage boy
working for tips at a friend's parents' party
in the twilight of some ancient Hollywood.
Why does it surface now, this visitation?
Because that Facel Vega would have fit in this garage.

DOCTORS

Dr. Lai's prophecy *You old man, it get worse*
has proved untrue: except for the aching joints
I feel much better than I did those years ago
thanks to the miracle of magnesium
and so as I wait in reception
for my annual physical with Dr. Chandra
I prepare to break the news to him
that I will decline the called-for colonoscopy:
First do no harm, my colon feels healthy as hell,
an organ, against all odds, at the top of its form.
Gratitude does not begin to describe my relief
for what health I have, I have been buying pens
on a binge trying to keep pace with the speed of ink streaming
seemingly nonstop from the Uniball,
so when the doctor's assistant calls my name
I am unprepared to discover I am thinner, lighter
than ever since whenever I weighed less
than I have in years, since I was young,
and the doctor says I should get on my bike
and notes the small cancerous spot on my arm,
We can burn that off with liquid nitrogen, he says
then sends me home without doing so, strangely cavalier.
Soon I will fast and make a fist for the phlebotomist
who will compliment me on my accommodating vein,
and I'll await news of the lipids, liplike globs of heartfelt
fat that could stop me in my tracks with their kiss of death.
Something will stop me soon enough, but for now
nothing can stop me, not even doctors.

REUNIONS

As we grow older we are more ourselves,
and this is evident at our reunions
when our illnesses are almost interesting,
the classmates the same only richer mostly,
possibly slightly dyed, uplifted, balding,
entrepreneurial, post-ambitious, fatter, skinnier,
more accomplished, almost finished
because what is left except to face each day
as if it is uniquely unrepeatable.
The school songs echo half a century later
only because you wrote them and they stuck
deep in the psyche to be triggered by the slightest
mnemosis, chronic disease of the memorious.
All those names from the class pictures,
each by now with an epic history,
or tragically abbreviated,
the faces forever fixed,
hairstyles frozen in black and white,
those Colgate smiles all but alive, amazingly the same,
standing on the front steps of the elementary school,
and the smaller faces in the rows of mug shots
on the glossy sheets are immortal
as the postage stamps of presidents
only more so in the remembering mind
educated in the changes of the years.
I search the retrofitted hallways
for traces of the old earthquakes,
flickers of temblors in the hearts of children.

BISHOP IN A BOX

Why does anyone want to be an author
when unsold books pile up ad nauseam,
titles of the famed and unknown equally obliviated
on remainder tables, limbo of tomes
en route to the library graveyards,
book sales of the afterlife, archival mausoleums,
storage lockers, small-town thrift shops. Words,
millions of words swirl through the overcast afternoon,
significance lost on distracted shoppers
occupied with their devices. The writing, then,
what is it for? Perhaps to leave your remains
in such a lovely case as one day some browser
may be drawn, may touch and be surprised
to find a feeling of what you were.

GARAGE ELEGIES 7

A broken dragon, one antler knocked off, with a tortoise shell,
of jade—little gargoyle paperweight purchased for nothing
by a kitsch collector in some Chinese antique shop—
waits patiently for something to weigh down:
a book order, a stray envelope, flotsam of correspondence
in the calm of the afternoon,
conscience wringing itself out with remorse
for long-ago deeds done or left undone,
invitations ignored or neglected, overtures overlooked,
seductions badly executed, every misplaced kiss and bungled
    embrace.
It is this way in perpetuity, impossible to let go
except in the whole present,
everything dragged in the wake that ever was mine,
always lost and stuck at the same time,
like my reserve across the room that night in the Café Central—
sabes quien eres. Each of you has haunted me ever since,
and I wish I could correct it but I can't.
And so I sit within sound of motorcycles gunning it up the coast
and moving vans across the street
and FedEx trucks cruising to drop things off
and some moron in a Honda speeding recklessly up the street
where I hope none of the cats are hanging out—
these background tracks are thematic, a score
unique to this document that mourns so much.

DENISE

Your face in the photo
is a young woman's,
beautiful, cool
with the subtlest of smiles
and radiant with calm confidence,
your trust in poetry's truth

untouched by its lack of cachet,
its distance from the mainstream's
muddy taste, because you knew
your song was sound,
and the lost masters easily found
in the opening of a book.

You drew power
from dry lines on a page, impossible
but somehow so, their music flying
into the psyche
to reassure, to fortify,
to please, like a lover's
touch.

When you encouraged me,
responding to my lyric overtures,
I confess my imagination made us
intimate,
though I was young enough
to be your son.

Now I am old
and you are gone,
and your gaze brings to mind

what got me
into this game, the promise of grace,
those patterns on paper
where being radiates.

WHAT IT IS

What do you make
of the record when the ink
runs out, the pencil is sharpened
to a disappearing point, typewriter ribbons
are nowhere to be had, and the juice is gone
the way of the poisoned wind.
Rhetorical, you say, and before the fact,
as evidenced by the ever-blackening page,
something to say, said, and taken aback
by its own, your own, imminent absence,
one's self taken back into silence,
in homage of and against which the traces
are trying to speak, and at a snail's pace
no race driver understands. Trying to keep up
with the mind's turns is a fool's game,
less fruitful even than philosophy,
as lost as poetry by a long shot. Losers
in a circle looking for reassurance
their pursuits mean more
than mutual support—yet out of such groups
some friend, some sad sympathy
may be mirrored in a fading page or face.
You have made some thing
of what wasn't and you wonder
what it is.

WHAT ELSE IS NEW

Every day brings new violations, fresh symptoms
of pathologies only vaguely understood by the experts,
the technicians of slumber, the pharmacists, the neuromani-
    curists,
prognosticators of personal apocalypse, out of which we opt
against all evidence—there must be more than the unwell
willing to testify, more than the sleepless,
the increasingly drowsy without relief,
the dizzy and the disappetized.
Even as it is writ it seeks to be scratched out
in the same ink, a failed erasure trying to right itself.
How could I have begun, I didn't know the first thing,
could not trace where the urge came from, only felt
some things must be said, spells spoken in tongues
beyond translation, off the lexicon where tumbleweeds roll their
    own
idiom of dust, wind, distant gunshots and false confessions.
The truth is no one knows who did it, and goes on doing
despite nobody's business, trying to nail down sounds
that don't hold still, won't even stand their ground,
disarmed as they are and not to be outdone.
They were held up
as examples of polyphony when one note
would've made all the difference, even a few
translingual syllables kissed off recklessly as at a wedding.
And so the broke laws, the compound boners,
the roles reversed and transgressed against long odds,
what the diagnosticians misinterpreted and understood,
each reach for the sky superseded by plexiglass.
What was had is lost, and what else is new.

INK IN MY SOCKS

Absent a tissue or scratch paper,
the best way to clean the little blob of ink
from the tip of the cheap ballpoint (pointlessly purchased
in the compulsive acquisition of office supplies
redundant in their multiplicity, more pens than Balzac burned
    through
fueled by caffeine) is to wipe it discreetly on your thick black
    sock
where even your wife won't see it when she loads the washer.
Such socks will serve as palimpsests of your false starts,
works in progress, footsteps into the labyrinth of the page
violated by your aimlessness, your search for a way clear
of your self-made maze. The blobs may build up a crust,
leave runes on your calves, your bald ankles—
black scabs, unintelligible squiggles for scholars to decipher
when they peel back the onions of your archives
weeping over what they don't understand.
Even what you left unsaid, smeared on your obscurest under-
    things,
will be seized upon for its clues to your lost truths,
the ones you couldn't bring yourself to write
because they'd prove you knew too much,
or your grief was cheap, or the soul you hoped was yours
didn't belong to you or anyone but was a floating wisp of smoke
adrift among equally flimsy receptacles of flesh
desperate to connect, to kiss what they couldn't keep.
All that ink downriver might have irrigated with its signature
the singular experience and wisdom,
the unique artistry of an individual,
but instead was blended with everything
and came to nothing.

WAITING ROOM

Tuesday afternoon and the clinic is busy,
walk-in sufferers mingling uneasily with appointed patients,
paperwork slipping out of folders onto the floor,
sterilized surfaces steadily humanized by the touch of contami-
    nated hands,
bacteria, viruses, cooties of all kinds swirling invisibly
to spook the as-yet uninfected, so sensitively exposed to every-
    thing.
That's why that woman is wearing a mask,
unless she is a bandit in drag, hussied up for a holdup
despite the security guard because what she has to steal is
    immaterial,
a few impressions, intimations of mortality, intuitions of
    inspiration,
mundane observations that open unexpectedly to reveal the
    eternal
and unstoppable, a robber's prerogative to appropriate whoever's
    drama
for his own scenario. What mirror is this in which you are
    looking
for what you don't know, what window looking out to the street
where vehicles are being pulled over by the Highway Patrol
for who knows what transgressions, the roads swarming with the
    driven
as they roll hopelessly hopeful to their rendezvous with obscurity,
their doctors and dealers in one drug, one dog or another
offering chemical or animal comfort to the afflicted.
What are you saying or are you merely waiting
to resume the usual, once the technician has peered into your
    brain
and determined how long you have, how much juice remains
to cruise through your synapses, how much more can you take

before the circuits are burnt and the lights go out.
This is why you have to keep your high beams on
and turn signals blinking, why the stadium lights must blaze
as the players circle the bases and make great catches and throw
    tricky pitches,
so the millions keep rolling in and their mothers can have their
    own houses,
and so you the spectator may enjoy the spectacle
for a few more innings of riches before extinction.

DEAD RINGER

Dead silent in the dead of night
at rest beside the lamp and the shut book,
the brass bell bought in the antique shop,
its clapper rewired so as to clang when rung,
wooden handle oiled by teachers' hands
who called their kids in from recess,
or a cook's fingers ringing in the family for a meal,
or the tired grasp of a convalescent calling the nurse for
    assistance,
has nothing to say at this hour when the wife is trying to sleep
and the mate is up late with nothing but thoughts
of what was forgot when he looked the other way.
The self-erasing blackboards of schoolrooms resonate
with bad boys' scrawls when the teacher had yet to arrive—
they had an idea almost, a joke, a blast of insurrection,
and soon they would be in the principal's office,
or prison, or be principals themselves incredibly
required to keep delinquents under control.
That bell could have called them to order
like a hammer, a gavel on the desk, an inkwell spilling
or spelling its secret sauce into the scribbles of distraction
and the bell could be banged to get the scribbler's attention
before a sentence of detention, or suspension, or expulsion.
It was in its day undoubtedly pedagogical,
the intelligent tone gives it away, but now it is dumb
because the night is long and insomniac beauties are in search of
    slumber.
How young we were when we could sleep
despite everything we didn't want to miss, and how deeply aged
of a sudden when we find ourselves wrung out, quiet in the old
    dark,
without a sound beyond the scratch of a stylus.

FIRING THE PSYCHIATRIST

Firing the psychiatrist is a sound idea,
the savings alone can buy several good dinners out
per session, and the drugs not taken
improve one's Weltanschauung immensely
as the chemicals percolate out of your system
and even the stoned fishes swimming in your excretions
feel their lightheadedness lifting and the ocean breathing
one small sigh of relief. You are human
nature and should spend more time outside
where the simplest landscaping, agapanthus purpling the after-
    noon
or a few succulents holding down the dust of a dry front yard,
can raise your gloom to tolerable levels and open your eyes
outward where the world is
beyond your brain. Soon you are not prescribed
but rather transcribing any anxiety into new forms
not recognized by the Desk Reference.
She herself agrees with no particular treatment
beyond good wine, a night on the town, sex as an aid to sleep,
and gratitude for the absence of disaster.
These warm days in early June are to be savored,
if only by strolling in the sun, thankful for legs to stand on.
The doctor orders no drugs, no worries, only awareness
of what is made real by the imagining mind.

BELL CURVES

The beauty of the bell
and its secret sound, still

within, hidden like a face
behind fallen hair,

put me under some odd spell
I don't understand,

hungry to hear its clang,
to ring it by hand

like old times, knowing
at the same time it is obsolete,

superseded by simulations,
simulacra of the actual,

which is what the bell holds
under its slow curves.

MINE

The grief must be got at
no matter how deep you must dig
or who gets hurt any worse than they already were,
unearthed bodies, skeletons too sexy to forget,
mines no matter who laid them, all of a piece
to shake loose primal dirt, so dark
even viral media won't touch it.
This is where false memories get mixed in,
fact-checkers be damned, there's more than evidence,
the eyewitnesses almost saw what happened
if they hadn't been looking the wrong way.
And so the excavators are summoned,
the sappers and the gravediggers,
the dusters of hard remains,
the men with headlights on their helmets,
even the painters scraping away and repainting
in layers over the primed images.
How far down must you drill
until hitting the first pain, or the vein
whose ore will enrich you when you own
what you don't know and you keep digging.

WAITING FOR THE ONE

Waiting for the one in Terminal 2
and she is decades overdue
and most unlikely to arrive on time
this time or ever again—
each slender profile dragging her bag
or toting her laptop down to baggage claim
appears to echo all those arrivals
from exotic assignments back to my embrace
and the riverbed of our curving rhythms
and sweet rapids of release.
Those long rides long gone return again
reflected in the buffed floors
where travelers trace paths
to contradictory destinations,
homes or hotels in harvest moonlight
bereft of forbidden fruit.
I hold the stone on my tongue
in hope some shred of flesh
remains to be tasted.

GARAGE ELEGIES 8

The nurses have arrived to comfort the afflicted,
bringing prescriptions and stories of their own ordeals
under the influence, and the suffering one takes it personally,
self-absorbed in a network of electric nerves.
This is what you were trained for in madhouses all those ages
    ago,
to negotiate altered states, inmates on incompatible trips
at odds with prevailing paradigms. You are now cool,
with help from your preferred medicine like everyone,
inoculated, and have learned to recommend your own regimens
according to existing conditions. The all-night tremors,
the shivering ripples, the heebie-jeebies of the mumbo-jumbos
whispering sweet-and-sour everythings in ears
where the cranio-sacralist has left her seeds
to sprout fresh imaginings in your flesh—
these phantom spirits know not what they speak,
they are subcutaneous yet without teeth, swirling like smoke
from the goofy ancestors' long-since-extinguished cigars.
We are doomed, no doubt,
but not yet, taking the waves day by day,
holding close at night the sweet warmth of the beloved
in whatever shape of lost sleep. Bad dreams may come,
and redeeming spells to expunge them, ineffective as elegies
to rescue the dead, yet almost magical in their mourning.

GARAGE ELEGIES 9

Extra Space Storage G205: Crypt of the Unsold Books—
a tale of horror for the unread author dreaming of mausoleums
where the neglected works patiently await the afterlife
from which they hope to escape.
Back in the world of the living they mean to casually amaze
like the slim gray fox who returns recurrently
trotting across the concrete past the garage
and over the back deck and uphill to hang in the yard
basking in the slanted shadows of the afternoon,
summer of luck hopefully opening for a moment—
pleasure in the penned lines long asleep revived
for the eyes of even one witness who may recognize
what they are, record of a life of little note,
no worldly consequence, immortal memory illusory in light
of a globe spinning out of control, oceans spilling over their rims
into the cities, animals no longer knowing where to go,
people displaced by disasters equally disoriented,
no time to read in a grid gone down in the dark.
Unlocked by an executor, the door to the author's tomb
reveals he was nothing but words in the first place,
his imprint Ecclesiastes Editions a vanity-of-vanities press
for those able to bribe their way into small print,
and to what end? To wait in the dark
for the evidence to be eventually unearthed.

SLEEPER WAVES

The pleasure in giving pleasure is the pleasure given
more than the gratification, the beauty of the enraptured face
greater than the pleasure taken. Words swirl
in the listening soul, something lifts or is lifted gently
as the beloved by the small of the back
pulled just a little way from the wall
where she might otherwise hit her head as she writhes
or reads your letters of love, evidence to be destroyed
lest anyone else witness. But in the cleansing wind of the river-
    mouth
where the bluff gives on gray sand and seagulls navigate north in
    groups
against prevailing gusts, you revisit or recreate
what you knew last night in some room
where what you sang to strangers almost mattered,
or a bed where with your bride you sweated sweetly
for a few blue hours. It's all mixed up, the songs
and the gulls' struggling upwind, your love's skin
and the ears receiving a ballad from the soul of the vocalist,
mere entertainment made somehow essential
amid the encircling miseries, symptoms of existence
for which any flash of light or whitecap
serves as a brief balm. These small waves of relief,
spasms of satisfaction, surges of birdlike grace
in the flesh or angels' commiseration in the mind,
say agony is not all, chaos is contained
when the spell is correctly said, pain is allayed
with a light touch in the right place. Ripping you out to sea
when you were looking the other way,
such waves can also be fatal.

ARTLESS WALL

No evidence of art on the blank wall
where an array of faces sprawled and spread
in changing layers over years of solitary composition,
a living collage of million-dollar dead
and equally dear as yet to be deceased,
their eyes and expressions alive
with everyday strangeness of the unexplained,
the fateful turns, sweet intimacies, inspirational
examples and edgy friendships. The corner stripped
of its expressive images, its colorful juxtapositions,
serendipitous rhymes and shapely sight-shifting lines
of association, is bereft,
abandoned for a box in some garage
where the pictures conspire to form fresh alliances
and, sooner or later, new revelations, pleasant surprises,
visual gratifications. What will never be seen again
is the surrounding space that gave that corner context,
the solo composer's studio where even now
his ghost sits writing this.

GARAGE ELEGIES 10

Report from Milosz on newsprint
clipped and mounted on a piece of cardboard,
glue plus light times time equaling a yellowish brown tone
of weathered paper, corrugation beginning to be revealed
in rippled vertical stripes behind the poem,
leans against a box on a plywood shelf
just low enough to be read, to remind you
of the contradiction, the worthless treasure
of poetry, "a most precious delusion."
Stacks of files wait patiently to be shipped to Indiana;
a lifetime of office supplies rests in cigar boxes,
banker's boxes, wine boxes, cartons
and coffins of all kinds, evidence for a trial
whose crimes went unnoticed, prints left undusted,
fingers inked and forgot.
Will the Goodwill want some of this stuff
to pass into the hands of phantoms happy to find a bargain?
Will collectors bid for it on ePhemera,
or will even second- and thirdhand shops rebuff such piles of
    obscure pages?
Who knows or cares but the primary carer
who nurses a strange grudge against his own good luck
and the turns for the worse everyone takes
with no exceptions. In search of solace
the muser has no clue what he is doing
and reaches out anyway hoping to find a hand.

MEDICATION MANAGEMENT

These drugs are good for you, I guarantee it.
Look what they've done for me.
Ever since the sales rep slipped some into the takeout coffee he
  brought me
I've felt better than a band of day traders in a manic market,
raking in the pills and the big bills like a winner at some green
  felt table
in Vegas on a Saturday night when nobody wants to sleep
and the all-night pharmacists are ogling the floor shows and
  hiring floozies
and have no relief to offer anyway. We are free
to manage our medication, swing our moods wherever we please,
be here now or then and there depending
on the time of day or place of worship,
in my case at the medicine cabinet where whatever moves
your madness can be muted and mined for my time
at premium rates. Side effects are beside the point,
you must have these tablets, these capsules, these transfusions
to soup you up and make you somewhat less monstrous,
more Jekyll and less Hyde, better repressed.
Trust me, my soup is hot, I am a doctor.

GARAGE ELEGIES 11

Langorous afternoons in late July,
the kind when the day's warmth brought sweaty
sweethearts cycling uphill to your sunny aerie,
cool breeze swerving through the rustic rooms
above the brook now silent in summertime, are history
and ever present on the Westside decades later.
The reflector flashes with pale blue light
glinting off the bay promiscuously in unforgettable abundance,
and reflects on current quietudes amid the agitations,
the domestic riptides, the wild rides of connubial confusion
when the shared bodies sicken inevitably together
even though only one is infected.
Such genius is contagious, the long embraces never ending
even when parted long since, the beds in the same hearts
even when separate. Wind chimes next door remind
the dove on the wire to call your attention to every sound,
not an adjective or adverb in sight, nothing but nouns and verbs
to be heard for miles. An oddly outdoor desk is witness to a
    street
redeemed only by its Japanese maples and birches and migrating
honeysuckle, miscellaneous succulents doing okay in the drought,
the anomalous magnolias. These trees, these fleshy leaves
making the most of the dry sky, those sirens
on Highway 1 a short walk away
are what you need most, or almost as much
as those athletic girls so long ago.

GARAGE ELEGIES 12

They come in sets, these waves you love swimming in,
riding, especially when they could kill you any second,
break your neck with a slam or drive you under for longer than
   you can take
or deeper into what you don't want to know
than you have time to write, the nerve to report
with truth, as you drown or save from going down
some skinny woman too beautiful to take your hand
for help. And there you are,
reaching for a grip that could pull you under
but won't because you want to live in spite of everything
mean and insane, everything chaotic and catastrophic,
claustrophobic, everything conspiring to exhaust you.
Because you must stand for the lazy man
too laissez-faire to be stirred from his leisure,
must fight for doing nothing and doing no harm.
What you are doing you don't know and it doesn't matter
but it must help you endure
the present tension.

TATTOOED LADIES

The circus has come to the supermarket,
where the young mothers strolling their toddlers are
even inkier than I am, their pale limbs drilled with designs
that will last a lifetime. What will their children do to be
    rebelliously
deformed—dip themselves in vats of invisible ink?
Hack off extremities in order to be fashionably disabled?
Drive spikes through their heads?
I wish my meager marks were that indelible, readable
across a parking lot where everyone is equally domesticated,
compromised by the confines of their shopping carts.
It's too late for me to be mural material,
my skin is starting to sag and my melanin
is already black and blue with race, with bad moods,
with melancholical tendencies unwarranted by objective
    conditions,
with Ashberian feints and false confessions
even Helen Vendler couldn't decipher,
coded mash notes left by old loves whose names I forgot,
a whole history of lost kisses left in private places
yet revealed in just such common light as anyone can see if they'd
    look.
So I am looking now, to see for myself what traces are left of a
    life on paper-
thin tissue of talking flesh and eyelids tonight that can barely
    keep up
with the changes of generations. Obsolete before my time is out,
I inscribe myself as obviously as I can
in order to beat the odds of oblivion.

BEDLESS IN BEDLAM

All the madhouses are maxed out,
no beds in the whole empire because of the Dread epidemic,
so the panicked patients are stacked in the hallways
while the young interns from Special Weapons and Tactics
make their rounds and the masked nurses mop up the spilled
    spirits.
VIDEO CAMERA NOT IN USE says the sign
by the red eye high on the wall, a relief for one
whose underwear needs to be changed. All the changes are
    accelerating,
mood swings driven by bad news, massacres,
natural and unnatural disasters, presidential debates,
each accident of fate a plot twist to thicken the skin
of anyone who wishes to stay sane.
Sane, *shmane*, as long as you're healthy,
but what if the mind has a mountain that's blown its top
and knocked passersby off their rockers.
Meanwhile in the dark steakhouse at lunchtime
a club sandwich is interrupted by a man lost in the last century
looking for a public telephone, and the kind patron at the bar
hands him a device for letting his wife know
he'll be late to the ER. These conveniences alleviate
some of the symptoms they create, sensations of brains
nervously networked together so all the world's psychic sewage
circulates promiscuously until everything is infected.
In the windowless rooms with sickening light, technicians
with beeping machines on wheels take vital signs
of horizontal people flattened by information.
So the bedless ones must settle for Bedlam instead,
and adjust to disorders they didn't request
when they filled out their forms to be born.

AN ANDALUSIAN SMOOTHIE

Not Lorca the charismatic cabaret singer,
nor Alberti who slipped his tongue unsolicited into his transla-
    tor's mouth,
nor the handsome and sexually reckless and finally brokenhearted
    Cernuda,
nor tubercular Aleixandre with his ice-blue eyes—
none of these suave operators can touch the taste,
on a Mediterranean August afternoon,
of summer's sublime cool soup chopped by hand
and sipped in solitude with a Rodrigo guitar concerto for
    accompaniment.
The liquid salad is music to my lips, tomato cucumber onion
    garlic
sweet red pepper lettuce a slice of bread a dash of olive oil
and a few drops of balsamic vinegar, the mixture blended
with salt, some sprigs of parsley added for a twist, or a touch of
    lemon—
such immense pleasure in simplicity, such easily swallowed
    Spanish medicine
transcends salsa, beet borscht, even fresh oysters with their
    lascivious implications.
Amid pandemic chaos and mayhem, a calm oasis
whose terroir is utterly local and exotic at the same time,
tinged with the tears of flamenco singers and phantom aromas
of orange blossoms, patatas bravas, magnolias and calamares.
How lucky to be alive amid the agonies
and still be able to savor a cup of gazpacho.

SEPTEMBER HEAT

Night hangs lightly
on the end of a warm weekend,
sleeves lost to the sun and evening shining coolly on naked arms,
though the coolest person on the patio has on his summer jacket
   and hat,
the better to distinguish himself from the nubile clientele.
How odd to be older than you ever imagined,
dozens, scores of years a blur in the long prologue,
preparation for the magic act of vanishing
while all other appearances persist in continuing
as you take your last sips of liquid gold
almost as delicious as a kiss.
These delusions taste deep,
as if steeped in truths as real as those lips were once.
What came undone then is what undoes you now,
something lived and lost
impossibly because it lingers always.

SO LONG, F. A.

Your daughter is listening
so I can't use the kind of language
you deserve (though she knows the words)
as we try to find someplace legal to scatter your ashes
in Santa Cruz, where your dad ended up in the Royal Hotel
and you had to pick up after him.
Are his remains around here someplace,
or long since gone with the wind after the scars he left
and you were eighty-sixed from civilization because your rage
at what he'd done kept getting you into fights in bars with other
    drunks.
You even tried to choose me off one time
when I stopped after my second beer
and you took it as a personal insult.
That morning on the river when I woke up
with your shotgun in my face—your idea of a joke—
and your overcoats with the big pockets for shoplifting,
and your midnight dives into Goodwill boxes
in search of merchandise for the flea market,
even our sordid and strangely tender threesomes—
twice, with different women—and your tough-guy loyalty
and letters to the editor in my defense
and offers to kill whatever enemies—
Fred, our friendship is inexplicable except for poetry,
and here I am like family sending you off into eternity
where you and Bukowski are having a few brews
before duking it out in the alley over who had worse luck
and toughed it out.

FLOATER

Something has come loose in my left eye
and tracks my glance as it roams the rolling flames
of coastal ice plant, invasive, plaguing the landscape
with its succulent beauty saluting the passing pelicans
cruising the cliffs, the kelp beds, the last swells of September
crashing in the coves, smoothing the wet sand
below the curves of the drive where police cars
and panel vans with business logos painted on the sides
roll also, rhyming with the waves
and the plants and the boats offshore and the skimming birds
and the whales unreal in their wild scale so close to the street
where people stop to prove they saw
by catching an image in a magic box
where all is shrunk to a screen
the size of this page
where I too try to seize what I see
and save it in a book to stash in my jacket pocket.

GARAGE ELEGIES 13

What wetness is this
moistening an autumnal afternoon
with drops of fine drizzle and thoughts
of the sweet center of her now lost in other mists,
the mind's, time's, seasonal reminders of other falls
when your truths were one in the long prologue
to present gifts and griefs, devastations and desolations
out of which rise swampy aromas of old cologne,
or is that the smell of her skin
blended with yours?
Nights and days you slept in the same dream
as if for all time, a moment prolonged more for its pure present
than such an afterlife as this yet somehow perennial,
reappearing at irregular intervals tricked by a climate
trying out new temps at odd times for just such surprises,
simple astonishments of the daily retrospectacle
too subtle to be noticed by most.
But you, least likely to succeed
of her whole alumni association,
veteran of brilliant embraces who failed
to retain what you learned, notice every lost thing
swimming past almost invisibly under a gray sky
and can scarcely explain its private writing
or scratch it out. It stays
to say how rich you are, even now,
with what remains of your fortunes.

ANONYMITUDE

for WLM

Misplaced in our respective centuries,
we're missing everything, my friend,
so obscured by ambitionlessness we slouch toward No Way,
that out-of-the-way roadhouse where even the open mike
is out of order and the jukebox busted so we have to sing
for ourselves and scratch rhymes on coasters
blurred by weeping brews of long-gone bards
whose books are out of print because they were never in.
This is the only refuge left for us because the new masters
are fighting for tenure and staking out turf
and we are collateral damage of the drones,
those missiles arcing like grave rainbows across horizons
beyond our reach. The postal service is all we have left
to transmit our old-school odes and epistles,
our epigrams and elegies, each a unique sheet,
our tablets postmosaic in their smashed eloquence.
We can scarcely tell the poseurs apart, so thick on the ground
and skilled if indistinguishable in their success,
and the authorities are not worth questioning.
Too old to rebel, we are causeless
because our enclosures are not contagious
and we are unplugged. Here's where the acoustics get good
and we think we can hear some trace of our strangeness
echoing across Texas like dry lightning.

ADVERSARY

for, and after, Gary Young

I found six toadstools sprouting from my father's corpse.
I had forgotten I had left him there to rot.
In one hand he clutched a decomposing hundred-dollar bill,
the same one he had given me for my bar mitzvah
and taken back because I wasn't Jewish.
His other bony claw was clamped around his dick
or a twig from one of the apple trees I'd been pruning.
My sons looked at each other and rolled their eyes.
An osprey cackled high overhead.
Son of a bitch always has the last laugh.

GARAGE ELEGIES 14

Ya get tired from doin' nothin'.
Ya don't know what the hell to do to kill the time.
Two sentences spoken by an old man in need of a shave
in an elevator in a Market Street hotel
in San Francisco half a century ago
to an eighteen-year old alone on his first road trip
echo now out of nowhere in the ears that overheard
and wondered at the strange world opening that summer
before his opening eyes.
Doing nothing is what poets do
in order to do the something of their dysemployment,
but even such a fertile void is filled with nothingness
and the nagging negative space of a vast absence.
Whom do you cite as an expert on this gloomy truth.
How far do you go to find that same old guy
idling away his last depressing days.

GARAGE ELEGIES 15

The idea that libraries last is illusory.
Look at Alexandria. And even without fire
the other elements erode the documents,
eat and delete the best-laid pages,
hollowing out the record helter skelter,
erasing even some of the old skeletons
though their bones do tend to outlast all
but the most memorable poems.
So when I was moving out of my last life
I left whole walls of books for the newlyweds moving in,
knowing I would miss those bound friends
but my new walls are smaller
so the nonessential volumes would end in storage
or sold or donated, never more mine anyway
the way they were when we lived together alone.
Even the salvaged treasures are stacked
in liquor boxes in this garage
and neither Borges nor Eco can read into them
mystic linguistic superpowers of print
which spreads its viruses sneakily through time
infecting with its matter-of-fact physicality
the very space the virtual displaced—
no, they do not traffic in transcendental hygiene
but collect subtle dust blowing through the cracks
from Mission Street and the delicate shit of insects.
Nevertheless they will see the light sometime,
perhaps in this lifetime, and so they are kept
on ice, kept closer than old
loves you felt you couldn't live without.

GARAGE ELEGIES 16

I was a ridiculous rich kid but it wasn't my fault.
By luck of the draw I entered the world
just as my father was starting to make his fortune
and my mother ascending the entrepreneurial stage
by way of the business that lifted all our boats—
ladies' swimwear from a Latter-day Saints designer,
luxuries of the leisurely in those rich years after the war
when factory workers had swimming pools in their yards
and executives' kids got cars for their sixteenth birthdays.
Mine was a comical Pontiac, powder blue, a convertible,
which I kept immaculate the better to impress my dates,
nice girls from good families, and others from south of the tracks
who were a little faster though to me it hardly mattered,
I was ignorant and all I wanted was kisses.
It wasn't such a stupid ambition
despite my oil-slicked hair and sporty styling.
I had to become a hippie to kill that kid,
but look, half a century along he lives in this ink
and laughs at my effort to save him from something
neither of us can name.

MY GYM AT MIDNIGHT

Rilke is running on the treadmill,
Camus is climbing the StairMaster like Sisyphus,
Kafka is curling dumbbells to build his biceps,
Borges is *smoking* on the stationary bike,
and Beckett is bench-pressing his bony weight.
I work out here for an hour every night
smelling the sweat of the immortal modernists,
Pound and Gertrude Stein sparring upstairs
knocking the blowhard horseshit out of each other,
their trainers furiously taking footnotes,
Wallace Stevens on the rowing machine,
Marianne Moore in the corner combing her mother's hair,
and Jimmy Joyce doing Chinese eye exercises
the better to get a glimpse of Homer's hardware.
All these bards are in surprisingly good shape
on Saturday night with nothing better to do
than press their pens as if pumping iron
to build their bodies to endure eternity
beyond the reach of their imaginations.
I come because I can't get a date either
and can think of nothing else to pass the time
than push these stupid weights around in circles,
put one foot in front of the other fast enough
not to fall off and crack my skull on the floor,
force my sagging flesh to try to firm up
before it's too late to say what I saw
when my eyes were still in the game
and my mind was sound.
My iPod plays the same songs as stream through the brains
of these musclebound masters chasing the same records
as the ancients, belaureled brows and sinewy limbs
gleaming under a moon aloof and buffed

beyond and above it all as Robert Graves.
Hart Crane is peddling Lifesavers like a cigarette girl,
and is that Bukowski handing out energy drinks?
I can't keep up with these fitness freaks;
I'm going home
to bed.

WHAT HAPPENED

What happened to that poem I wrote in Berkeley
on my portable Olivetti in MLK Park
on a summer morning twenty years ago.
I charged the customer a dollar
because we were raising money for *Poetry Flash*
so I was writing "poems in a flash"
and she happened to be the first one of the day.
She gave me three words I don't remember
and I started typing, the lines coming easily and rather sexily
because I didn't care how immortal it was or wasn't,
I was just typing as fast as possible, letting it write itself
to be ripped from the carriage and given away
never again to be seen, at least by me.
For a first draft it wasn't bad, it caught something
of the sunny weather, June, the solstice, a Saturday morning with
    coffee
and kisses, not even noon, the day beginning, a sense of the
    possible,
a card table with a typewriter and a poet in a folding chair,
fingers not thinking but traveling lightly over the keys as
lines arrived in the typing mind, no pauses to revise
but a sprint to the last line and a poem
just like that, writ to order and delivered on time.
She took the paper from my hand and read
and registered astonishment, delight, excitement.
I'd scrawled my name illegibly under the text.
Will this be worth something someday? she asked.
It's worth something now, I said—
a dollar anyway.

NEITHER HERE NOR THERE

Aloft, left coast below
on the right, I am in flight
in a small jet, escapist

in the way of one who flees
or has fled what is never left,
like family scattered, even dead

with years, who stay, sticky
with space in folds
of the brain, remaining

faster than friends, pulling back
even as you streak in time
through wide sky as if

removed, free of the grave
forces pulling down. Down
and back anyway

against what drives ahead,
almost abstract, except
for the lines and folds in familiar

faces grown strangely aged,
old, near ancient
if not so immediate,

these presences. What absence
are you trying to eradicate
if not the same one

as always and inevitably, she
who has stayed so long
as to haunt your every journey

away.

THE WAVES ARE MORE BEAUTIFUL
WITHOUT THE SURFERS

The waves are more beautiful without the surfers
and the woman without the computer.
Laptops have come between me and so much love
the damage can't be calculated.
Devices that grow the brain into alien dimensions
begin to possess their possessors in that universe
and the rest is infection with circulating viruses,
promiscuous intercourse, so unlike the slowly cresting swells
rolling in from the west just barely peaking in places
skimmed by a sole pelican. Give me that view all day long
over a screen unless the screen be the Japanese kind
behind which a woman is undressing.

SIRENS

A flock of sirens has occupied my bluff,
a half dozen girls in white slips, clothes in a pile nearby,
huddled together as if for warmth or a photograph
in fifty-degree weather in front of the bench
where I like to sit and look across the iceplant
out to sea under a gray sky today
and a few cool drops of stray rain.
Am I hallucinating such a lovely vision,
an old man's imagination working overtime,
or did these sirens place themselves just so
for my amazement, their bodies shimmering,
or shivering, naked limbs aflame
with fair-skinned fire in the January light,
strollers past pretending not to notice,
except for me, smiling in astonishment
at such a gratuitous gift
on a grim Sunday.

WHAT LIGHT BREAKS

Gazing gloomily into his private tide pool
Narcissus is knocked into the indifferent ocean
by a sneaky wave big as a building—
but who cares about his or anyone's going under
in the face of natural facts, no scarf thick enough
to protect the neck of the condemned, his bad mood
embodied in one last song, mostly a melody alone
with too-late-to-matter lyrics, the singer
another loser trying to turn his bad luck on its head
for a twist of surprise
pleasure for a change.
Soloists under berets to keep their bald heads warm
are barely musicians anymore, aged
faint echoes of ourselves fading into the fog
as we slide with our lyres ever deeper
into grief with no light at the bottom
to reveal how far we've come from the arms
and open mouths of those who planted these blues
as they kissed us into existence.
It always comes back around
and down to this, the lost lips
that launched us on this journey to the end
of a tunnel into a night so long
and short it goes by forever
in a flash.

HUNGRY NOMAD

The nomad hunts for lunch,
unused to his condition
as one who has escaped
a sentence yet to be measured
in its ongoing ordeal,
and finds only cafés
where no one will take his order
and so he circles hunger
hoping some waitress
will show up with a sandwich
before he starves. He could
do without the food but not
her face, which echoes others
in its rhyming eyes and
almost familiar lips.

AT OLITA'S ON THE WHARF

A monk with backpack peers over the rail
to snap a shot of a seal with his smartphone,
shaved head gleaming in the late light of early spring
end of the day, last days of spirit, flesh fading,
sea beasts breathing their last.

I sip a skinny margarita at Olita's
where Amber has failed to arrive for our dinner at 5
and at 5:45 I am driven to write for lack of anything better,
one drink down and a taco delivered by a tattooed waitress in her
    place.
Waiting for nothing anymore, a blank slate long since erased,
replaced by faintest traces of whatever was, now always gone.

How unilluminating this temporary escape,
hastily scribbled on a page that saves the author
from solitude, sun cutting through the shades intended to shield
    his eyes
from blind rage at fate, what takes one from luck
to the Gypsy's curse or evil eye of age,
the sole option to early demise.

What a strange deal, this hard bargain
with language and life that you mistook
for one and the same and were left with neither,
or mere shreds of what you thought
meant by their sweet promises.
Instead, this.

LOOKING AT THE OCEAN

The alcohol fog or gloom feels strangely good,
grim reapings of increasingly gray days,
dark in spite of the spring sun. What is writing
but a way of wringing something from nothing,

like the sound of another solitary
strumming a guitar on another bench,
another seeking some small consolation in sound.
How could there come to be so little left

and why does it take tequila to uncork this pathetic melancholy,
truth too blue to be told, the musings of nobody
worth noting or noticing. You have been reduced to a cliché,
something you have opposed since you were old enough

to know the difference, and now you've become
what you most disdained,
one of the defeated.

And yet what luck
to be on a bench looking at the ocean
on a mild evening in March.

BUMS ON BENCHES

Bum asleep on a bus-stop bench,
me on a park bench looking at the bay,
gray day in Surf City, sun failing to burn
through overcast, fog between here and Monterey,
a stray helicopter chopping northwest into the haze,
lazy undulations through the kelp beds, no swell
to speak of, no waves.

Man on the bench is unshaved, sunburned, drunk,
unkempt, piece of a newspaper by his feet, filthy clothes,
no self-respect, like me
confessing what nobody wants to know,
but who cares, I have nice shoes, new laces,
a shower at home and a sick spouse,
all the pleasures of bobohood
and unsold books to burn,
so who is worse off—
he, to be sure.

I am privileged to sit
and watch shearwaters skimming by
inches above the silver, which moves sinuously,
subtly, like skin sweetly writhing under a lover's touch.
I flunked out of Love U.,
failed to understand,
that's why I'm out here nodding on a bench
at the West's end, a wild man with no idea
how he wound up this way.

GARAGE ELEGIES 17

Got to get back in the garage
and crank out some more elegies,
the bodies pile up and where have you been
to kiss them off and pull them back for a few sentences,
just long enough to miss them again
like the whale whose back you glimpse for a second
before it vanishes again, hard-to-fathom
evidence of the unbelievable.
The humpbacks beggar disbelief,
as do the pictures of the departed
decorating these shelves whose waves of faces
rhyme with the swells a mile away
sweeping you off in a riptide of gratitude
and regret, waves of clichés as well,
no new thing to say, just another derelict with a sob story.
Not swervy enough, too much grief,
same old nothing doing
when what's done is done
and you live with it ever after.

GARAGE ELEGIES 18

The sound of thought, of figuring out what you think,
of your brain on ink, your voice talking to itself,
your song taking shape on the page,
who would find time to engage in such wasted pursuits
when they could be doing something
or gazing at their personal device,
same thing as you with your striped book,
artifact of museum displays under glass,
library archives unexcavated, memories of the aged,
fading. Those old sages are endangered, like whales
and anyone else with a brain that's gone to his head,
imagining he's immortal as death hasn't landed yet,
or just because what else is there to do
but see what's in front of you, listen for its
rustling murmur like the voice of your best love,
long gone yet still right there, evidence
you lived, how amazing is that. What use
to remark on this, or sit looking southwest
with your neck caressed by a cold breeze,
you might even call it wind, what history is gone with
and here with at the same time,
like birds skimming the kelp beds on a gray day.
It is all you can do to feel it all.

GARAGE ELEGIES 19

The sound of speed is my brother's grunts
as he fucks Miss Checkered Flag,
the babe who is the payoff for finishing first,
and groans of my other brother growing up quick
only to land with four kids in the suburbs.
My sister was a teenage bride, had babies,
then her husband gave her a new face and left,
and she ended up on the Upper East Side with a son of a bitch
who finally had the decency to die, and now she is free
but seventy-three and feeble.
I'm the one whose job it is to remember and report back,
what my dad didn't understand and Mom took offense at,
on defense at all times to defend the fact
she could not be wrong,
and so we go on talking to ourselves and to shrinks
trying to figure out where it went before it's too late
to know the difference because it's all over
and you had your chance and that's that,
a smudge on the page where you smacked a fly
because its buzz bugged you and
you had bigger sounds in your head,
but it was you.

NUDE BEACH

Nobody on the nude beach, too cold, overcast hugging the coast,
spring wind on time but the gloom is unusual, its dark tone
mirrors blue moods, mythic imaginings, journeys of initiation
where the original ordeal is reenacted and the boy
emerges as a man, or the other way round, or neither
as he is eaten alive by ants,
and sand flies are biting his eyes,
and the kelp smells bad at low tide,
just beyond range of middle-schoolers toting backpacks
trudging back to the bus, sand in their shoes
to analyze in class for the ways it slips through the hourglass
leaving them aged at day's end,
deceived by sex ed.

GARAGE ELEGIES 20

Pitched past pitch of grief,
Hopkins most eloquent of depressives
made music of his darkest of dark nights,
just as the white butterfly, delicate as anything,
transgresses the driveway on a sunny Sabbath
when everyone but the rabbi is celebrating the long weekend.
He is bragging humbly of the studied wisdom
whose wind has slammed the door on his claim
to an inside route to the absolute,
he confesses to the congregation
that he is as baffled as they by the twists of existence,
they are on their own and even unnameable gods
can't help—but try to be kind anyway.
Far from the synagogue a garage may serve
as a sanctuary, a space for the faithless,
boxes of spare prayers in storage
where they have stashed what they can't say.
No wonder, the words ran out and didn't come back,
like dead friends who forgot to say goodbye—
though some called on the last day, just to chat.
Ben Jacob, son of Jake, who spent his Sabbaths at the track,
debates with nobody whether or not
he should watch the ballgame on cable, listen all day
to the sirens, or go outside and play with the recreators—
none is a persuasive waste of time
on a day when graduates are walking dazed with their diplomas
into the blind glare of debt and desire's promises.
What do you mean
that you can't explain
in a newspaper column,
what isn't so simple
as to be summed up in 600 words.

Look at the spring growth on the honeysuckle,
the puffy weeds blowing seeds recklessly wherever,
the parched succulents hanging on for a drink,
believing in some relief.

30 DAYS TO BETTER ENGLISH

30 Days to Better English,
weather-warped paperback
left on a bench near West Cliff
as if meant for me by an unseen benefactor,
is lost on me after thirty days
even though brought home for my reference shelf
beside *The Romance Writers' Phrase Book*
to which I refer whenever I'm trying
to seduce an admiress, bless her heart
and that breakaway bodice she wears
whenever she reads.
But thirty days is too long to help
improve my translingual skills,
those kisses left on the battlefield
where I earned my rusty medals
and ended up hors de combat
like a mercenary pacifist who got paid to refuse
to take up arms other than those
of her who used him up
and left him defenseless.
He has forgotten whole dictionaries,
got his Greco-Roman grammars
garbled, his etymologies
misplaced, mnemonic devices
disremembered like the faces of all those babes
who failed to replace her.
They did fill in a few blanks,
were pleasantly multiple choice for a few moments,
but never caught his tongue with the same fluency.
And so my sentences don't measure up
in decades of decline
from those speechless peaks.

ON BOOKSHOP SLOPES

Gary Snyder jumped off the shelf
and onto the floor at my feet
in the poetry section—
     surely a sign
        from graybeard uncle
to pay closer attention
when I'm reaching for Mark Strand collected poems
     with cover art by Steinberg
and knock Gary's off
so that's the one I must buy

and take to the terrace of the art museum
which used to be exercise yard of county jail
where inmates hung on the chain link
shouting to pedestrians below on Front
     asking for cigarettes
        or some babe's attention
and open and read a few poems
and am reminded of Gary's clarity
his teacherly wit and scholarly street smarts
     to impart skills around the homestead
        or library or campfire or mountaintop
or jumbo jet streaking him from one continent to another
to transmit what he knows
     to those who care

I'm not sure whether what I care
matters anymore
or what if anything I have to teach
but Gary's in good shape for someone his age
and he can still write
so he's a role model

pages flap in coastal breeze
the succulents breathe
the sculptures in this garden look comfortable
but the fountain is off and I miss
       its watery sound

GARAGE ELEGIES 21

He was living in the backhouse behind his mother's place
and pretending it was an office and that he was an executive,
his desk a reflection of what he had seen on TV,
blotter, telephone, gun in the drawer,
an imaginary universe where he was boss,
much the same way I sit here envisioning a view of the bay
where the big pickup across the street is parked on July Fourth.
I'm feeling patriotic in a funny way,
having just read the Declaration of Independence,
great political poem, on the back of *The New York Times*
and at the same time aware of the ironies,
but the writing in that document is dynamite,
a verbal bomb to knock out the tyrant's teeth.
The cat in the driveway is not impressed,
he trots away unaware of the historic date,
though I expect he dislikes fireworks and was awakened last
    night,
as I was, by little explosions banging in the street.
Hideous beige ranch house behind the white pickup
hides a sad-looking old woman in a housedress
who receives a lot of packages from UPS
and puts out all three of her big trash and recycling bins
like clockwork every week. The dude whose pickup that is
shares the adjacent place with other young men of large physique
whose surfboards sometimes stick out of their truck beds.
Across from them the guys are working on their cars in Spanish
and girls are coming by in shorts bringing stuff for the barbecue.
These traces are more or less true to life and no less lacking.

FROM THE ELEGIAC TO THE FUNEREAL

From the elegiac to the funereal,
my mood is increasingly engloomed,
demoralized by mortality
and historical convulsions that beg the question of the plausible.
Eyes examined, dilated, shot by machines and spat out into
   sunlight
with clip-ons and a baseball cap,
I am barely able to shop for groceries
or read the *Times* but I can see the news is bad
and there's so little I can do,
no matter who's president or whose book gets reviewed.
What if all these words add up to what I think they do,
what then, and what does it matter?
Looking across at the recycling bins in the library,
carefully labeled—paper containers, compost, landfill—
something appears in order, even if only waste.
Otherwise the tissue of civilization is flimsy,
chaos leaking through from outside,
the barbarians not beat as Lipton wrote, much less holy,
unless you count the bible slappers on the attack.
No, it's just you and the hooligans,
every homeless hard-on for itself and no relief.

GARAGE ELEGIES 22

How do the new dead blur
in the streaks of tears down the bereaved faces
grieving in disbelief the sudden impossible losses,
what forms must mourning take to serve their memory,
what plain joys and pleasures measure up to the absences,
the missing persons.
Consider the beautifully robust young bodyworker
at the farmers market, tall and strong
with the flushed cheeks of the recently orgasmic,
whom you mistook for another brilliant girl
you've never met and you struck up a conversation
and now she is in your office working on your wife—
what kind of luck is that?
Or lunch with another woman elegant in her silvering,
or a friend whose marriage is almost as strange as yours,
or coffee with a couple of lovely lesbians
worthy of Sappho's lust in their fresh appetite for the physical,
all evidence that amid the neverending atrocities,
buds of breastlight, flashes of eyegleam
elevate heartbeats and remind you of what is everpresent
even while forever out of reach and beyond recovery.
That sound she made when she came,
your first taste of her tongue,
what touching her felt like—
these are the pleasures you never lose
even though you will never know them again.
You must notice every platonic signal of correspondence,
every sexy nuance, and when a fox looks in
through the French doors as you are eating breakfast
you must trust it is a gift and not a mirage,
small measures of grace against the enormous horrors.
Jack Gilbert, one of the unstrung lyre lovers

who left one delicious light green brick of a book,
wrote somewhere that we must savor what sweetness we are
   given
to overcome the refugees' sufferings, to counterbalance,
counteract the victims' violated bodies, the shredded lives.
The cruelty of the aggrieved cannot be comprehended,
and the tenderness of affection never denied.

RIVER LOVERS

My river ran off,
after all our curved swirls and rippling swells
and sweet rapids of release, one rainy night she slipped out of bed
and fled through town leaving a trail of heartaches in her wake,
a flood of suitors who didn't rise to her level,
logs and ripped-out roots from way up the valley
smashing into our bridges and washing up on the beaches,
evidence of our devastation,
               egrets taking flight in one last flash
        of the beauty we knew, the grace—
I had to call the corps of engineers and even they
couldn't contain her, the wetlands of our floodplain spreading
    again
with every storm, it felt so good we couldn't hold the pain
and so these birdlike cries until the quake or the wildfire
                rakes through the ruins to take what little
   remains.
The climate has changed, it scarcely rains anymore,
the stream has thinned, like an elderly vegan
who needs a burger and a shake,
        and yet in its desiccated state it displays its ducks
and delinquent gulls and random great blue heron
and tough and slender rushes in the shallows
sadly sipping last season's watery kisses.
       Now I wait for storms to fill the reservoirs
           and look for shreds of myself—
evenings across from the railroad trestle
when we smoked in the dark and looked upriver
at the lights reflected in the water and the shadowy shapes
of the mountains, or the walk I took along the bike path
when I was leaving town for the last time
following my bliss to a bigger river on the other coast,

or pausing on the footbridge after lunch
        on the way back to jury duty
to gaze at the crimeless calm of the trees
and smell the breeze blowing in from the Boardwalk
with corndogs and cotton candy on its breath.
                A little wilderness snakes through town
and who even notices but those who have next to nothing
and who need a place to chill or do their illicit deals
or hide from a world that disdains them
        to write their confessions no one will read
or drown their losses in a fog of intoxication
or make love under an indifferent sky.

AWAITING MY WREATH AT THE BEVERLY WILSHIRE HOTEL

The truckload of laurels should pull into Valet Parking any
    minute
and dump them on the red carpet for starving poets
to season their soups with for a few years.
Between a Mercedes Benz and a Maserati
my wounded Subaru is parked with dignity on Rodeo Drive,
washed this afternoon so the sun's reflection off its silvery surface
will flash in the blinded lenses of the paparazzi and enable my
    escape,
more skilled and sneaky than Diana's,
from their invasive glances.
May female gazes find my attire sufficiently fetching
to attract their admiration and let the bartenders for social
    responsibility
shake their cocktails with aplomb in the heart of deepest Holly-
    wood.
Though the fragrant leaves are scratchy on my brow
and the olive oil gleaming on my tanned skin feels slightly
    slippery,
I can keep my feet on the marble floors of the ballroom
and won't let glory go to my head because tomorrow I'll be
    nobody again,
like Odysseus pulling the wool over the Cyclops eyes,
those cameras trying to fix us for eternity.

YOUNG RUNNERS

In the afternoon light of Ocean Avenue
the cross-country team is running through Palisades Park,
a flock of sweaty sixteen-year-olds burning off
the burgeoning juices of adolescence
until the heavier aching sets in,
chemicals and magnetic fields of mating
forcing bodies to fetch and find each other,
which is when the losses begin, the bad news rising
after the bliss, but what if there's more than this
and even marriage amounts to less
than what the vows meant when you believed they were round as
     gold
until death came to fill your love full of lead and it started sinking
way out past the lifeguards, beyond saving range,
and so you had to seek higher land where you might meet
some widowed soul or lost winner whose languages you share,
whose tongues you speak as if translating thoughts
otherwise unsayable, know what I mean?
I wish I could whisper it some other way
but it escapes me, like what I should have said
when I had a chance and couldn't because it was all too true,
it would've changed everything and then what—
another round of love roulette, of sudden roses opening
and found faces closing in for the kiss.

GARAGE ELEGIES 23

The sloped floor makes these lines run downhill
along lines of least resistance under the power lines,
what rain there was washed into the bay and windchimes ringing
a few doors up across the street.
I have come to the garage again in search of tax returns,
pre-qualification for change of location,
some other place to look at the street and muse,
uselessly, on wheels of cars and bicycles and chairs
going nowhere, turning like verses in the ground,
like tinkling things in the wind, sound without mouths
to say it, my mother's breath on the couch.
It is a steep drop to the plastic barrels
facing the street for the city's trucks to flip
in the crashing dawn, and it is straight down
to Hades where Bukowski is playing the horses
and Fat Jack is in his box and all's right with the underworld.
Meanwhile here the same birds circle,
same silver Porsches speed down the street,
same cats stroll nonchalantly around the garage,
glancing my way with a tone of tolerance.

GARAGE ELEGIES 24

What if this garage is not the last castle
and some aerie or other calls oddly out of the dark,
with or without wings, talons, flesh-tearing beak,
an unrecognizable cry that sounds like a siren, Calypso
chased by police for going too fast on the freeway,
running red lights and driving reluctant travelers mad
with song. What if the sound meant rooms with views
and a new love in every bed and a wrenching away of love
from the familiar, illness intervening, deadly jealousies,
insurmountable resentments, worst cases made persuasively
by seasoned advocates who've seen everything
and know the jury will never make up its mind and will be hung
like portraits of aristocrats who look idiotic in their dopey
      dignity,
as if Goya had caught them with their masks down.
Widows with retrofitted faces wave from upper floors
of mansions and balconies of unaffordable condos
that they are your last chance, sweet flirts
with husbands tracking every touch of their smartphones,
nothing-whisperers who resemble muses
dictate lyrics you don't quite get—
must you take them down, or seriously?
Late, when your eyelids start to droop
and every stray car going by wakes you up with its rumble
and couples are heading back to their hotels
to couple happily before returning to the grind,
you must listen for hints of where the fork not taken
may yet beckon.

LANDSCAPE WITH TREES AND FREEWAY

The church steeple has to go, and the fog of exhaust fumes,
but keep the streaming lights at night, and those eucalypts
in the foreground, and in the distance the profile of dark hills
and ridges, and let the footbridge to the post office
serve as your link to civilization as you paint your way
out of the corner you've constructed
from romance and the accidents of desire.
Looking northeast into wintery space
you must recalibrate and renovate your fate
in what could be one last round
before your soul is recycled,
so you might as well place an ocean over there
where, weather permitting, you can sketch pelicans
or take a lunch break on a bench.
You can see only as far as the edge of the canvas
including everything in sight,
from the alleyway under the window to the fluffy clouds
full of everyone's information, and as you stroke on
the slow-drying shapes and colors with a soft brush
or slash with your pocketknife
or delicately trace with a stray eyelash
the face of her who led and left you here,
you want to be sure her cryptic figure
is unnoticed by those who never knew,
who never saw that face in summer light, up close,
and felt themselves possessed by such a gaze.
But for those who know, look closely between the traffic
and the railroad tracks and the mountains
and the downtown rooftops and the coast,
and see if you can discern what the artist found
and lost, save for what is revealed here.

GRANDSON

Two weeks in the world
he is ill at ease
at odds with existence

crying confused
his mother's breast
removed for a minute

softly I assure him
I understand
it's tough out here

calming a little
he quiets down
opens his swimmy eyes

in my direction
as if to ask
how has this happened

one day he was nothing
then a blob in a dark belly
now this

I say it's true
it's a dirty trick
but we are these forms

changing every day
breasts beyond reach
our bodies disbelieving

distress on our faces
protesting our losses
words no consolation

small courage coming
in a voice close by
soft sound of hope

STEPHEN KESSLER's poems, translations, essays, criticism and journalism have appeared over the last fifty years in hundreds of literary magazines, newspapers, anthologies and books. His translations of Luis Cernuda have received the Lambda Literary Award for Gay Men's Poetry, the Harold Morton Landon Translation  Award from the Academy of American Poets, and the PEN Center USA Translation Award. His version of *Save Twilight: Selected Poems* by Julio Cortázar received a Northern California Book Award. He has edited numerous magazines and newspapers, most notably *Alcatraz,* an international journal; *The Sun,* a Santa Cruz newsweekly; and *The Redwood Coast Review,* four-time winner of the California Library Association's PR Excellence Award. He is also the editor and principal translator of *The Sonnets* by Jorge Luis Borges, and the author of a novel, *The Mental Traveler.* For more about Stephen Kessler, visit **www.stephenkessler.com**

TITLES FROM BLACK WIDOW PRESS
TRANSLATION SERIES

A Life of Poems, Poems of a Life
by Anna de Noailles. Translated by Norman R.
Shapiro. Introduction by Catherine Perry.

Approximate Man and Other Writings by Tristan
Tzara. Translated and edited by Mary Ann Caws.

Art Poétique by Guillevic.
Translated by Maureen Smith.

The Big Game by Benjamin Péret.
Translated with an introduction by Marilyn Kallet.

Boris Vian Invents Boris Vian: A Boris Vian Reader.
Edited and translated by Julia Older.

Capital of Pain by Paul Eluard. Translated by
Mary Ann Caws, Patricia Terry, and Nancy Kline.

Chanson Dada: Selected Poems by Tristan Tzara.
Translated with an introduction and essay
by Lee Harwood.

Earthlight (Clair de Terre) by André Breton.
Translated by Bill Zavatsky and Zack Rogrow.
(New and revised edition.)

*Essential Poems and Writings of Joyce Mansour:
A Bilingual Anthology.* Translated with an
introduction by Serge Gavronsky.

Essential Poems and Prose of Jules Laforgue.
Translated and edited by Patricia Terry.

*Essential Poems and Writings of Robert Desnos:
A Bilingual Anthology.* Edited with an introduction
and essay by Mary Ann Caws.

EyeSeas (Les Ziaux) by Raymond Queneau.
Translated with an introduction by Daniela
Hurezanu and Stephen Kessler.

Fables in a Modern Key by Pierre Coran.
Translated by Norman R. Shapiro. Full-color
illustrations by Olga Pastuchiv.

Fables of Town & Country by Pierre Coran.
Translated by Norman R. Shapiro. Full-color
illustrations by Olga Pastuchiv.

Forbidden Pleasures: New Selected Poems 1924–1949
by Luis Cernuda. Translated by Stephen Kessler.

Furor and Mystery & Other Writings by René Char.
Translated by Mary Ann Caws and Nancy Kline.

*The Gentle Genius of Cécile Périn: Selected Poems
(1906–1956).* Edited and translated by
Norman R. Shapiro.

Guarding the Air: Selected Poems of Gunnar Harding.
Translated and edited by Roger Greenwald.

I Have Invented Nothing: Selected Poems
by Jean-Pierre Rosnay. Translated by J. Kates.

The Inventor of Love & Other Writings
by Gherasim Luca. Translated by Julian & Laura
Semilian. Introduction by Andrei Codrescu.
Essay by Petre Răileanu.

Jules Supervielle: Selected Prose and Poetry.
Translated by Nancy Kline & Patricia Terry.

La Fontaine's Bawdy by Jean de La Fontaine.
Translated with an introduction by
Norman R. Shapiro.

Last Love Poems of Paul Eluard.
Translated with an introduction by Marilyn Kallet.

Love, Poetry (L'amour la poésie) by Paul Eluard.
Translated with an essay by Stuart Kendall.

Pierre Reverdy: Poems, Early to Late.
Translated by Mary Ann Caws and Patricia Terry.

Poems of André Breton: A Bilingual Anthology.
Translated with essays by Jean-Pierre Cauvin
and Mary Ann Caws.

Poems of A.O. Barnabooth by Valery Larbaud.
Translated by Ron Padgett and Bill Zavatsky.

Poems of Consummation by Vicente Aleixandre.
Translated by Stephen Kessler.

Préversities: A Jacques Prévert Sampler.
Translated and edited by Norman R. Shapiro.

The Sea and Other Poems by Guillevic.
Translated by Patricia Terry. Introduction by
Monique Chefdor.

To Speak, to Tell You? Poems by Sabine Sicaud.
Translated by Norman R. Shapiro. Introduction
and notes by Odile Ayral-Clause.

MODERN POETRY SERIES

WWW.BLACKWIDOWPRESS.COM